THE MYTH ABOUT SEX

Exposing the Aftermath of Valentine's day

BY

DANNY GEORGE AWAIKO

Danny George Awaiko

LEGAL DISCLAIMER

Published in Nigeria by
DANGOFE PUBLISHING HOUSE
3 Duenta Street, Abuloma,
Port-Harcourt, Rivers State Nigeria.
TEL: +23408063689774, +23408056738866
Email: dannygeorge002@yahoo.com

ISBN: 9781793049445

TABLE OF CONTENT

Dedication

This book is dedicated to everyone who wants to abstain from sexual immorality.

ACKNOWLEDGMENT

First of all, I acknowledge God in whom I move, and breathe and have my being. All I am today is because of him. I am forever grateful.

I appreciate my wife Glory Danny George for being my no 1 fan, and for believing in me.

I also want to appreciate my spiritual father, Arch-Bishop Sam Amaga the presiding Bishop of Foundation Faith Churches world-wide; for giving me the platform to serve.

I also want to appreciate Prof. Francis Bola Akin-John, Rev Joe Ojekudo, Rev Emmanuel Olusanya, Dr. George Anselem, and Rev Godwin David for their fatherly support. And a big God bless you to Mrs. Ibifaa Asawo (Journalist) for editing this book.

Introduction

There is a great misconception on the subject matter of sex. So many persons believe a lot of wrong theories and articles they read about sex. In the first place sex was created by God and not by the devil. God talks about sex a lot in the bible. Sex is God's wonderful creation and should be practiced within the confines of marriage, which is God's will.

Furthermore, sex has been so misused and perverted by the devil and the world that the impression has been created that sex is ugly and sinful. That's why during Valentine's Day, so many evils are committed in the name of celebrating love.

In the pages of this book find out some of the myths and realities about sex.

Chapter One

The Myth about Sex

Myths are legends, fairy tales and half-truths. They are handed down to us by our forbearers. They are believed without question and proper research as to their veracity. Myths are widely held believes that are difficult to change from. Many of those myths we live by disallow us from seeing reality. Myth tends to becloud one's judgment and sense of reasoning. With particular reference to sex, myths have not allowed many to face the reality and truth of things to know about sex. In this chapter we shall be examining some of these myths and the reality so that our perspectives can be enhanced and balanced.

MYTHS 1

Sex is a way of expressing your love to your boyfriend or girlfriend.

REALITY 1

There are different ways of expressing love, such as buying a gift, cooking a nice meal, etc. another way of expressing love is having sex with your husband or wife. Romantic behavior such as kissing, petting, fondling, is not meant for sinful boyfriend and girlfriend relationships but for properly married couples.

MYTHS 2

Sex is the fastest way to force a man to marry you

REALITY 2

As a young girl submitting your precious body to every "Tom Dick and Harry", for sex, because you want them to propose to you; will not always work. This is because majority of these men only see sex as fun and can never use it as a criteria to propose to you. Moreover men will never trust you because they feel that you are also sleeping around with other men, just like you did with them.

MYTHS 3

Sex is a game

REALITY 3

Sex is not a spectator event. If you think people are applauding you because you go about deceiving and luring people to bed, think again because you have another thing coming.

MYTHS 4

Sex is a sin and was created by the devil.

REALITY 4

Sex was created by God and not the devil. Sex has been so misused and perverted by the devil and the world that the impression has been created that sex is ugly and sinful. On the contrary, sex is God's wonderful creation. When practiced within the confines of God's will, sex can only lead to more joy and peace in the marriage.

MYTHS 5

Sex is a means of survival

REALITY 5

Having sex with different men as a young girl, for the purpose of making money is called prostitution. Prostitution leads to destruction, you will lose your integrity and even contact STDs, which may likely lead to your death.

MYTHS 6

Sex is the cheapest way to punish my husband.

REALITY 6

It is common for a wife to be uninterested in sex due to emotional stress, sicknesses, fatigue, or just to punish the husband for reasons best known to her. If this persists for too long, the natural fallout is break-up, infidelity or polygamy. Both couple should not defraud, cheat or torture each other by denying or depriving each other of sex.

MYTHS 7

Sex is competition

REALITY 7

You don't need to mimic or listen to the stories about the sex life of other people. You might end up becoming promiscuous while you are trying to emulate them. The only remedy is to understand your own spouse. Sex is not about scoring 10 out of 10 for your performance, it is about having fun with your partner and show care.

MYTHS 8

Teachings on sex by a single person is a good idea

REALITY 8

Experience they say is the best teacher; but, you cannot read books and gather some imaginary facts to lecture people on a subject matter like sex. You must be in the system of marriage so you will be confident enough to back up your claims with concrete examples. I know a lot of persons will not agree with me on this, but that is the hard truth.

MYTHS 9

Having sex with your fellow man or woman to woman sex is not a bad idea.

REALITY 9

It is a crazy idea for you as a man to have sex with your fellow man, or as a woman to have sex with another woman. You are either a gay or a lesbian. However, God created Adam and Eve not "Adam and Steve". Take a look at the male sex organ and the female sex organ; you will discover that God created the male sex organ for penetration into the female sex organ, for the purpose of reproduction, pleasure, release of tension etc. So it is ironical for you as a mere mortal to change that divine order.

MYTHS 10

Sex is a negotiating tool for business or a contractual agreement

REALITY 10

Some persons have used their spouse to seal up business deals in the past because of greed for money. This act is ungodly and unwarranted, as you might end up losing your loved ones to this erroneous act.

MYTHS 11

There is nothing wrong in stimulating my genital organs in order to receive sexual pleasure.

REALITY 11

Having sex with you is called masturbation; it is not good and also ungodly. It is a very dirty habit and also irritating. I have already treated the subject of masturbation in chapter ten of this book.

MYTHS 12

Sex is the real thing on Valentine's Day.

REALITY 12

During Valentine's Day, so many evils are committed in the name of celebrating love. Men go all out to spoil their women and some of the women feel they have to pay back in a way by giving him what he wants. Some feel if a guy spoils you with gifts, you owe him, reducing Valentine's Day to a cleverly orchestrated business transaction: you give me things I give you sex. For most people, sex is an important part of Valentine's Day. Whether or not people are in a relationship, sex seems like a big part Valentine's Day package.

Before you decide to take off your clothes for a few minutes of fun, think again and again about the implication of your action.

Implications

1) Sexually transmitted diseases are for real

STDS don't have respect for age, colour or race. No matter your age, you could still get infected. It only takes having sex one time with an infected partner to get infected yourself. Most people with STDs are not even aware they have it. Love is a beautiful thing, STDs are not. Don't put yourself at risk.

2) You are immune to pregnancy.

If children are not in your near future, you should think twice before deciding to roll underneath the sheets. Every year, thousands of young girls end up with pregnancies they did not plan for and they are abandoned by the men who claimed they loved them in the heat of passion. When you are left to face the consequences alone, you are faced with two options, keep the baby or abort it. Which will you choose?

3) Condoms are not perfect

You might be thinking you can prevent STDs and pregnancy with condom but it's a known fact that condoms are not 100% safe. Remember they can break.

4) You don't want to live with regrets

You don't want to wake the next day wishing you did not do it. It might be fun while it lasts but you might end up with more regrets afterwards.

5) Sex is not love

Don't get it twisted. Just because someone has sex with you doesn't mean they love you. Ask the prostitutes who sleep with different men for a living. Majority of the time people have sex just to have sex and not for love.

Chapter Two

What God Says About Sex

Sex outside marriage is having a devastating effect on the world today. Most people including Christians choose to ignore God's instructions concerning this matter. A lot of pastors choose to ignore teaching God's instructions and unfortunately society is crumbling under the weight of this sin.

In this chapter we will explore few things about what God concerning sex.

God Limits Sex within the Confines of Marriage

Marriage should be honored by all, and the marriage bed kept pure, for God will judge the adulterer and all the sexually immoral. **Hebrew 13:4(NIV)**

You Sin Against Your Own Body When You Commit Sexual Sin

Flee fornication. Every sin that a man doeth is without the body; but he that committed fornication sinneth against his own body. ***1 Corinthians 6:18***

Your body belongs to Christ not to a harlot

Know you not that your bodies are the members of Christ? Shall I then take the members of Christ, and make them the members of a harlot? God forbid.

What? Know ye not that he which is joined to a harlot is one body? For two, said he, shall be one flesh. ***1 Corinthians 6:15-16***

Sex is an exchange of life

For the life of the flesh is in the blood: and I have given it to you upon the altar to make atonement for your souls: for it is the blood that makes atonement for the soul. **Leviticus 17:11**

You Defile Your Body

What? Know ye not that your body is the temple of the Holy Ghost which is in you, which ye have of God, and ye are not your own? For ye are bought with a price: therefore glorify God in your body, and in your spirit, which are God's. **1 Corinthians 6:19-20**

Repentance

Ask God to forgive you from all sexual immorality. Sexual sin is not just a sin against you; it is predominately a sin against God. Are you a man or a woman? Your body is not for sale. God forgives easily, just talk to Him about it and resolve in your heart never to do it again. You can attend any bible believing church and narrate your ordeals to the pastor or you can connect with me via email or my phone contacts. God bless you.

About The Author

Danny George Awaiko is a young dynamic Revivalist, a Preacher, a Motivational Speaker, and a man who loves the Holy Spirit. He also shares his insight with singles. He is an author, and has written several inspirational books like: 10 Steps To Become A Champion, Checklist For Savings And Investment, 21 Ways to Identify False Prophets, 7 killing D's Of Destiny, 7 Catalyst of Revival, 24 Secrets of Worship, 7 spirits fighting the church, Holy Spirit My Best Friend and many others.

For 13 years he has impacted on so many youths in different higher institutions, which led to him winning the Aaron and Hur's award as his first award in 2008. His first book, "The Secret Is Out", has reached out to many lives. He is a mindset coach, a personal development speaker, and a financial analyst. Danny volunteers to aid the campaign against the spread of HIV and pre-marital sex. He is a conference speaker. Danny leaves in Port-Harcourt,

Nigeria and loves writing, reading, fitness and travelling.

Connect With Me

Thank you for buying and reading this book, please remember to leave reviews and connect with me on social media platforms:

Email: dangofe002@gmail.com

Facebook: @ Danny George Awaiko

Twitter: @dannygeorge

Instagram:@Danny George Awaiko

Mobile Number:

_+23408063689774, +23408056738866_

Other Books By: Danny George Awaiko

1. The Secret Is Out

2. Destiny Plucked Out Of Fire

3. Holy Spirit My Best Friend

4. 24 Secrets of Worship

5. 21 Ways to Identify False Prophets.

6. 7 Killing D's Of Destiny

7. Checklist for Savings and Investments

8. 7 Catalyst of Revival

9. 7 Spirits Militating against the Church.

10. 10 steps to become a champion.

11. Sex Without Knowledge

EXPOSING THE VULNERABILITY OF THE GIRL CHILD
Sex Without Knowledge
CHECKLIST FOR SAVINGS AND INVESTMENTS
SEVEN SPIRITS MILITATING AGAINST THE CHURCH
10 STEPS TO BE A CHAMPION
THE SEVEN KILLING "DS" OF DESTINY
EXPOSING THE SPIRIT OF DELILAH
DANNY GEORGE AWAIKO
EXPOSING THE ACTS OF FALSE PROPHETS IN THE 21ST CENTURY
21 WAYS TO IDENTIFY FALSE PROPHETS
DANNY GEORGE AWAIKO
DANNY GEORGE AWAIKO
HOLY SPIRIT MY BEST FRIEND
SEVEN CATALYST OF REVIVAL
DANNY GEORGE AWAIKO
Experiencing the Casting Crown event in the book of Revelation
24 SECRETS OF WORSHIP
DANNY GEORGE AWAIKO